BEATLEMANIA
1967-1970

CONTENTS

TITLE	PAGE
ACROSS THE UNIVERSE	5
ALL TOGETHER NOW	8
ALL YOU NEED IS LOVE	2
BABY YOU'RE A RICH MAN	11
BACK IN THE U.S.S.R.	14
THE BALLAD OF JOHN AND YOKO	17
BECAUSE	20
BEING FOR THE BENEFIT OF MR. KITE	22
BLACKBIRD	24
CARRY THAT WEIGHT	26
COME AND GET IT	28
COME TOGETHER	31
A DAY IN THE LIFE	34
DEAR PRUDENCE	37
DON'T LET ME DOWN	40
EVERY NIGHT	46
THE FOOL ON THE HILL	43
GET BACK	50
GOLDEN SLUMBERS	48
HELLO, GOODBYE	53
HEY JUDE	59
HONEY PIE	56
I AM THE WALRUS	62
INSTANT KARMA	66
I WILL	72
JULIA	69
LADY MADONNA	74
LET IT BE	79
THE LONG AND WINDING ROAD	82
LUCY IN THE SKY WITH DIAMONDS	76
MAGICAL MYSTERY TOUR	84
MAXWELL'S SILVER HAMMER	86
MAYBE I'M AMAZED	89
MOTHER NATURE'S SON	92
OB-LA-DI, OB-LA-DA	94
OH! DARLING	97
PENNY LANE	100
REVOLUTION	102
ROCKY RACCOON	105
SGT. PEPPER'S LONELY HEARTS CLUB BAND	108
SHE CAME IN THROUGH THE BATHROOM WINDOW	114
SHE'S LEAVING HOME	111
STRAWBERRY FIELDS FOREVER	116
THAT WOULD BE SOMETHING	118
WHEN I'M SIXTY FOUR	125
YOU NEVER GIVE ME YOUR MONEY	120

COPYRIGHT © 1980 ATV MUSIC PUBLICATIONS
ALL RIGHTS RESERVED

ISBN: 0-89524-110-2

All You Need is Love

G D Em D G D7 D9 D7
Love love love Love love love
D7 G
D.%. al Coda
Coda
G A7sus
All you need is love
D7 G A7sus D7 G B7
(Spoken) All to-ge-ther now All you need is love (Ev-ry-bo-dy) All you need is love
Em G C D7 D11 G
Love That is all you need That is all you need That is
(That is all you need)
Repeat till fade.

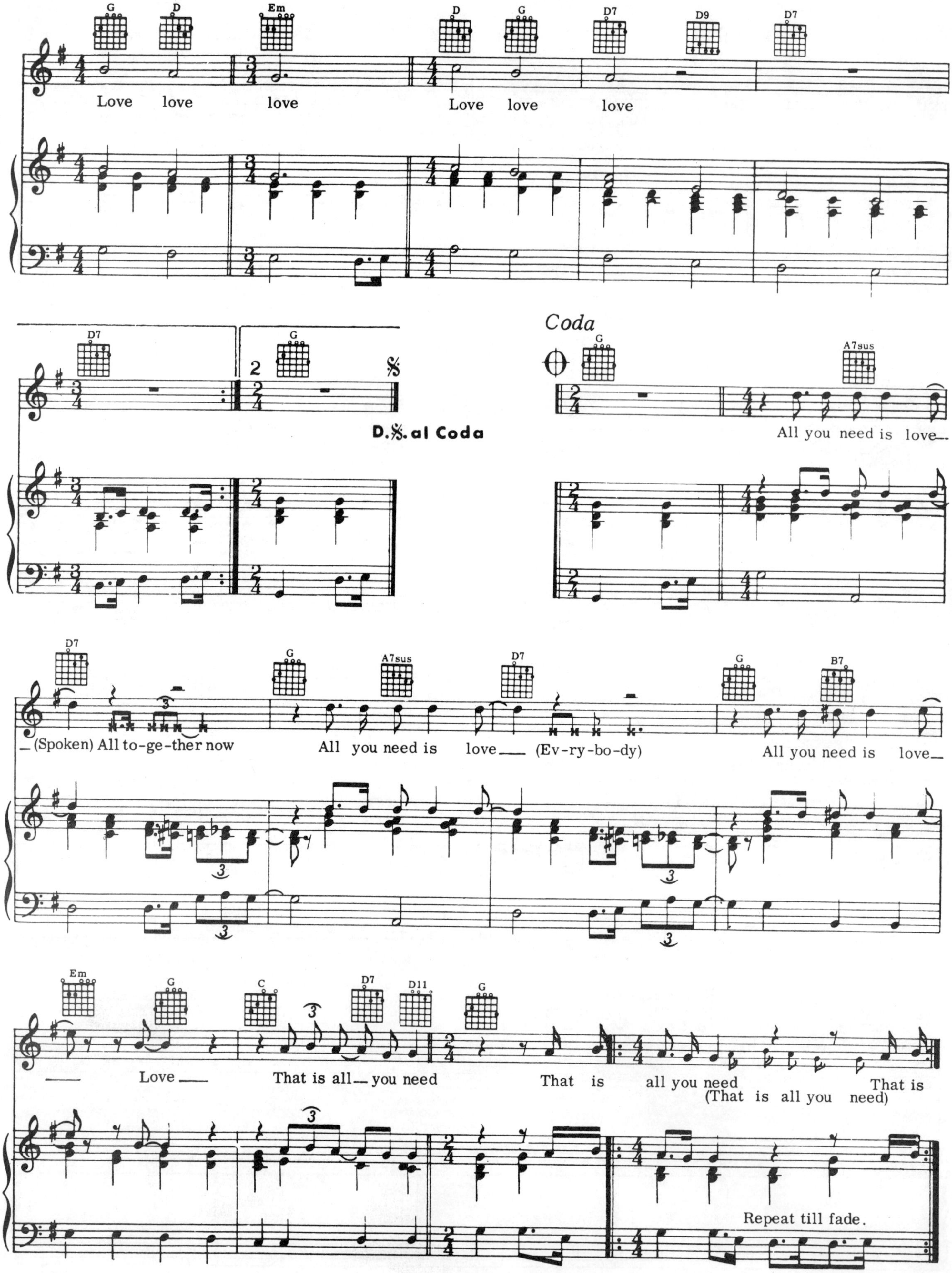

Across the Universe

All Together Now

Words and Music by
JOHN LENNON and
PAUL McCARTNEY

Copyright © 1968 NORTHERN SONGS LIMITED, 24 Bruton Street, Mayfair, London W1X 7DA, England
All rights for the United States of America, Canada, Mexico and the Philippines controlled by
MACLEN MUSIC, INC., c/o ATV MUSIC CORP., 6255 Sunset Blvd., Hollywood, Calif. 90028
All Rights Reserved

Baby You're a Rich Man

Words and Music by
JOHN LENNON and
PAUL McCARTNEY

Copyright © 1967 NORTHERN SONGS LIMITED, 24 Bruton Street, Mayfair, London W1X 7DA, England
All rights for the United States of America, Canada, Mexico and the Philippines controlled by
MACLEN MUSIC, INC., c/o ATV MUSIC CORP., 6255 Sunset Blvd., Hollywood, Calif. 90028
All Rights Reserved

Back in the U.S.S.R.

Words and Music by
JOHN LENNON and
PAUL McCARTNEY

Copyright © 1968 NORTHERN SONGS LIMITED, 24 Bruton Street, Mayfair, London W1X 7DA, England
All rights for the United States of America, Canada, Mexico and the Philippines controlled by
MACLEN MUSIC, INC., c/o ATV MUSIC CORP., 6255 Sunset Blvd., Hollywood, Calif. 90028
All Rights Reserved

Because

Words and Music by
JOHN LENNON and
PAUL McCARTNEY

Come and Get It

Come Together

Words and Music by
JOHN LENNON and
PAUL McCARTNEY

Copyright © 1969 NORTHERN SONGS LIMITED, 24 Bruton Street, Mayfair, London W1X 7DA, England
All rights for the United States of America, Canada, Mexico and the Philippines controlled by
MACLEN MUSIC, INC., c/o ATV MUSIC CORP., 6255 Sunset Blvd., Hollywood, Calif. 90028
All Rights Reserved

32

A Day in the Life

Words and Music by
JOHN LENNON and
PAUL McCARTNEY

Copyright © 1967 NORTHERN SONGS LIMITED, 24 Bruton Street, Mayfair, London W1X 7DA, England
All rights for the United States of America, Canada, Mexico and the Philippines controlled by
MACLEN MUSIC, INC., c/o ATV MUSIC CORP., 6255 Sunset Blvd., Hollywood, Calif. 90028
All Rights Reserved

Dear Prudence

Words and Music by
JOHN LENNON and
PAUL McCARTNEY

Slow Tempo

1, 4. Dear Pru-dence won't you come out to play,
2. Pru-dence o-pen up your eyes,
3. Pru-dence let me see you smile,

Dear Pru-dence greet the brand new
Dear Pru-dence see the sun-ny
Dear Pru-dence like a lit-tle

Copyright © 1968 NORTHERN SONGS LIMITED, 24 Bruton Street, Mayfair, London W1X 7DA, England
All rights for the United States of America, Canada, Mexico and the Philippines controlled by
MACLEN MUSIC, INC., c/o ATV MUSIC CORP., 6255 Sunset Blvd., Hollywood, Calif. 90028
All Rights Reserved

Eb
Eb7
Abmaj7
Abm (maj7)
Eb
Eb7
day ha-hay - hay, The sun is up, the sky is blue it's
ski - hi - hi - - es. The wind is low, the birds will sing that
chi - hi - hi - - ld, The clouds will be a dai - sy chain so
Abmaj7
Abm (maj7)
Eb
Eb7
4th time to Coda
Db
Ab
4th Fret
beau - ti - ful and so are you Dear Pru - dence, Won't you come out to play,
you are part of ev - 'ry - thing Dear Pru - dence, Won't you o - pen up your eyes,
let me see you smile a - gain Dear Pru - dence, Won't you let me see you smile,
1.3.
Eb
Eb7
Abmaj7
Abm (maj7)
2.
Eb
Ab
4th Fret
2. 4. Dear
Bb
Ab
4th Fret
Eb
Ab
4th Fret
Bb11
Ab
4th Fret
Look a-round, 'round, ('round, 'round, 'round, 'round, 'round, 'round, 'round) Look a-

round, 'round, 'round, ('round, 'round, 'round, 'round, 'round, 'round, 'round) Look a - round.

3. Dear

Won't you come out to play.

Fade-Out

Don't Let Me Down

Words and Music by
JOHN LENNON and
PAUL McCARTNEY

Don't let me down, Don't let me down.
Don't let me down. Don't let me down.

Nobody ever loved me like she does, oo she does, yes, she does.
And if somebody loved me like she

She done me, oo she done me, she done me good.
I guess nobody ever really

Copyright © 1969 NORTHERN SONGS LIMITED, 24 Bruton Street, Mayfair, London W1X 7DA, England
All rights for the United States of America, Canada, Mexico and the Philippines controlled by
MACLEN MUSIC, INC., c/o ATV MUSIC CORP., 6255 Sunset Blvd., Hollywood, Calif. 90028
All Rights Reserved

do me,___ oo she do me,___ yes, she does.
done me,___ oo she done me,___ she done me good.

Don't let me down.

CHORUS 2

Don't let me down.___ Don't let me down.___ Don't let me down.___ I'm in love for the first time.___ Don't you know it's gon-na last. It's a love that lasts for-

To Coda

INTERLUDE

ev-er,⎯⎯ It's a love that had no past. Don't let me

down, Don't let me down.⎯⎯ Don't let me

down.⎯⎯ Don't let me down.⎯⎯ And from the first time that she real-ly

Coda

down.⎯⎯ Don't let me down.⎯⎯

The Fool on the Hill

Words and Music by
JOHN LENNON and
PAUL McCARTNEY

Fairly Bright

1. Day after day alone on a hill, The man with the foolish grin is keeping perfectly still; But nobody wants to know him, they can see that he's just a fool, And
2. Well on his way his head in a cloud, The man of a thousand voices talking perfectly loud; But nobody ever hears him, or the sound he appears to make, And
3. *(Piano Solo - Voice tacet)* .... Nobody seems to like him they can tell what he wants to do, And

Copyright © 1967 NORTHERN SONGS LIMITED, 24 Bruton Street, Mayfair, London W1X 7DA, England
All rights for the United States of America, Canada, Mexico and the Philippines controlled by
COMET MUSIC CORP., c/o ATV MUSIC CORP., 6255 Sunset Blvd., Hollywood, Calif. 90028
All Rights Reserved

44

Coda
Cm
Fm
Cm
Fm7
Fool on the hill sees the sun go-ing down, and the eyes
D7-9
in his head see the world
tacet
C
Dm7
spin-ning 'round.
C
Dm7
C
Dm7
Repeat ad lib till fade out

Every Night

Words and Music by
PAUL McCARTNEY

Moderately

Verse

Ev-'ry night — I just want to go out, — get out — of my head.
Ev-'ry day — I lean on a lamp post, — I'm wast-ing my time.

Ev-'ry day — I don't want to get up, — get out — of my bed.
Ev-'ry night — I lay on a pil-low, — I'm rest-ing my mind.

Ev-'ry night — I want to play out, and ev-'ry day — I want to
Ev-'ry morn-ing brings a new day, and ev-'ry night — that day is

Copyright © 1970 NORTHERN SONGS LIMITED, 24 Bruton Street, Mayfair, London W1X 7DA, England
All rights for the United States of America, Canada, Mexico and the Philippines controlled by
MACLEN MUSIC, INC., c/o ATV MUSIC CORP., 6255 Sunset Blvd., Hollywood, Calif. 90028
All Rights Reserved

do, oo,— oo, oo, oo.
through, oo,— oo, oo, oo. But to-night,— I just want to stay in and be — with you,— and be — with you.

Chorus

Oo, oo, oo, oo, oo, oo, oo, oo,— oo,— oo.—

Repeat and fade

Golden Slumbers

Words and Music by
JOHN LENNON and
PAUL McCARTNEY

F C Em Am Dm7
wake you when you rise; Sleep pret-ty dar - ling, do not cry,
G7 C Am7
And I will sing a lul-la - by. Once, there was a way to get back
Dm7 G7
home-ward. Once there was a way to get back
C Em Am Dm7 G7 C
home. Sleep pret-ty dar - ling, do not cry, And I will sing a lul-la - by.

Get Back

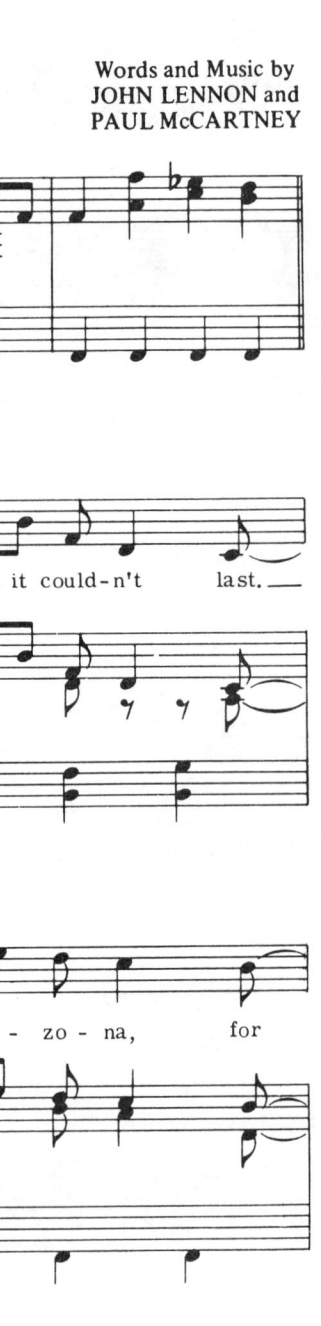

Words and Music by
JOHN LENNON and
PAUL McCARTNEY

Moderately (in 4) *(with a heavy beat)*

VERSE

Jo Jo was a man who thought he was a loner, But he knew it couldn't last.

Jo Jo left his home in Tucson, Arizona, for some California grass.

CHORUS

Get back! Get back! Get back

Copyright © 1969 NORTHERN SONGS LIMITED, 24 Bruton Street, Mayfair, London W1X 7DA, England
All rights for the United States of America, Canada, Mexico and the Philippines controlled by
MACLEN MUSIC, INC., c/o ATV MUSIC CORP., 6255 Sunset Blvd., Hollywood, Calif. 90028
All Rights Reserved

to where you once be-longed.____ Get back!____ Get back!____ Get back____ to where you once be-longed.____ *(Get back, Jo Jo)* Sweet Lor-et-ta Mod-ern thought she was a wo-man, but____ she was an-oth-er man.____ All____ the girls a-round her say____ she's got it com-ing, But,____ she gets it while she can.____ Get back!____ Get back!____ Get back____ to where you once be-longed.___ Get back!___ Get back!___ Get back___

to where you once be-longed.___

(Spoken:) Get back, Loretta. *Your mother is waiting for you.*

D.S. and fade out on Chorus

Wearin' her high heel shoes and her low neck sweater, *Get back home, Loretta.* Get back!

Hello, Goodbye

Words and Music by
JOHN LENNON and
PAUL McCARTNEY

Moderato

why you say good-bye I say hel-lo ___ I say high
You say yes ___
last only I say yes

You say low ___ You say why ___ and I say I don't know ___
I say no You say stop ___ and I say go ___ go go
___ But I may mean no I can stay till it's time to

go Oh no ___ You say good-bye ___ and
go Oh ___

I say hel-lo ___ hel-lo ___ hel-lo ___ I don't know
1st only Hel-lo good-bye hel-lo good-bye ___ Hel-lo good-bye ___

why you say good-bye I say hel-lo ____ hel-lo hel-lo ____ I don't know
hel-lo good bye hel-lo good-bye Hel-lo good-bye

why you say good-bye I say good-bye ____
hel-lo good-bye ____
Why why why

why why why do you say ____ good-bye good-bye ____

CODA
____ Hel-lo hel-lo ____ I don't know why you say good-bye I say hel-lo ____

Hel-lo ____ He-la ____ he-ba hel-lo-a cha cha

Repeat till fade

Honey Pie

Words and Music by
JOHN LENNON and
PAUL McCARTNEY

Ad lib

VERSE

She was a work-ing girl North of Eng-land way.

(Half spoken)
Now she's in the big time In the U. S. A.

And if she could on-ly hear me, this is what I'd say:

Medium Bounce

CHORUS

Hon-ey Pie, You are mak-ing me cra-zy. I'm in love, but I'm
Hon-ey Pie, My po-si-tion is tra-gic. Come and show me the

Copyright © 1968 NORTHERN SONGS LIMITED, 24 Bruton Street, Mayfair, London W1X 7DA, England
All rights for the United States of America, Canada, Mexico and the Philippines controlled by
MACLEN MUSIC, INC., c/o ATV MUSIC CORP., 6255 Sunset Blvd., Hollywood, Calif. 90028
All Rights Reserved

la - zy,___ So won't you please come__ home. Oh
ma - gic___ of your Hol - ly-wood song.___ You be-came_ a leg - end of the sil -
Will the wind_ that blew__ her boat a-cross_
ver screen,___ And now the thought of meet - ing you makes me weak_ in the knee.
___ the sea,___ kind - ly send__ her sail - ing___ back to me.

T - T - Tee,__ Oh Hon-ey Pie,__ You are driv - ing me fran - tic.__
T - T - Tee,__ Now Hon-ey Pie,__ You are mak - ing me cra - zy.__

58

Hey Jude

Words and Music by
JOHN LENNON and
PAUL McCARTNEY

Slowly

Hey Jude, _____ don't make it bad, _____ take a sad song _____ and make it bet-ter. _____ Re-
mem-ber to let her in-to your heart, _____ then you can start _____ to make it _____ bet-ter. _____ Hey

Jude _____ don't be a-fraid, _____ You were made to _____ go out and get her. _____ The
Jude _____ don't let me down, _____ You have found her _____ now go and get her. _____ Re-

min-ute you let her un-der your skin, _____ then you be-gin _____ to make it _____ bet-ter. _____
mem-ber to let her in-to your heart, _____ then you can start _____ to make it _____ bet-ter. _____

Copyright © 1969 NORTHERN SONGS LIMITED, 24 Bruton Street, Mayfair, London W1X 7DA, England
All rights for the United States of America, Canada, Mexico and the Philippines controlled by
MACLEN MUSIC, INC, c/o ATV MUSIC CORP., 6255 Sunset Blvd., Hollywood, Calif. 90028
All Rights Reserved

F7
B♭
Gm7
And an-y-time you feel the pain Hey Jude, re-frain, don't car - ry the world
So let it out and let it in Hey Jude, be-gin, you're wait - ing for some-
C7
F
F7
B♭
up-on your shoul - ders. For now you know that it's a fool who plays it cool
one to per-form with. And don't you know that it's just you Hey Jude, you'll do.
3
Gm7
C7
F
F7
C7
By mak - ing his world a lit - tle cold - er. Da da da da da da da da
The move - ment you need is on your shoul - der. Da da da da da da da da
1.
2.
F
da. Hey Hey Jude, don't make it
3

bad. Take a sad song and make it bet-ter. Re-mem-ber to let her un-der your skin, then you'll be-gin to make it bet-ter, bet-ter, bet-ter, bet-ter, bet-ter, bet-ter, Oh Yeh yeh yeh yeh yeh yeh yeh da da da da, Da da da da 'Hey Jude

Da da da da da da da da da da Hey Jude.

Repeat till fade with effects.

I am the Walrus

Words and Music by
JOHN LENNON and
PAUL McCARTNEY

I am he as you are he as you are me and we are all to-geth-er

See how they run like pigs from a gun see how they fly I'm cry-ing

Copyright © 1967 NORTHERN SONGS LIMITED, 24 Bruton Street, Mayfair, London W1X 7DA, England
All rights for the United States of America, Canada, Mexico and the Philippines controlled by
COMET MUSIC CORP., c/o ATV MUSIC CORP., 6255 Sunset Blvd., Hollywood, Calif. 90028
All Rights Reserved

A A7 D Fmaj7 G 3 fr. A
Sit-ting on a corn-flake___ wait-ing for the van to come___
Yel-low mat-ter cus-tard___ drip-ping from a dead dog's eye___
Sem-o-li-na pil-chards_ climb-ing up the Eif-fel Tow-er_
F B
Cor-por-a-tion tee shirt, stu-pid blood-y Tues-day man_ you been a naughty boy_ you let your face grow long_
Crab-a-lock-er fish-wife por-no-graph-ic priestess boy_ you been a naughty girl_ you let your knickers down_
El-e-men-t'ry pen-guin sing-ing Ha-re Krish-na man_ you should have seen them kicking Edgar Al-lan Poe_
C D D7 to Coda E
I am the egg-man Oh they are the egg-men Oh I am the wal-rus Goo goo g' joob
1. A A7 C D E A A7
Mis-ter cit-y p'lice-man sit-ting pret-ty lit-tle p'lice-men in a row___

C D A
See how they fly like Lu-cy in the sky see how__ they run__ I'm cry-ing__ I'm
D sus4 A E
cry - - ing I'm cry-ing I'm cry - -
D D7 2. E B A G F E B A
7 fr. 5 fr. 3 fr. 1 fr 7 fr. 5 fr.
ing Sit-ting in an En-glish gar-
effects
G F E F B7
3 fr.
-den wait-ing for the sun__ If the sun don't come_you get a tan from stand-ing in the English rain_

C D D7
I am the egg-man Oh they are the egg-men Oh I am the
E D A A7
wal-rus, Goo goo g' joob g' goo goo g' joob
Ex-pert tex-pert chok-ing smok-ers
C D E A A7 C
don't you think the jo-ker laughs at you?
See how they smile, like pigs in a sty, see
D A
how they hide I'm cry-ing
D. S. al Coda
Coda
E
wal-rus Goo goo g' joob g' goo
D C Bsus4
goo g' joob Goo goo g' goo g' goo goo g' joob joob Ju-ba ju-ba ju-ba
Repeat till fade

Instant Karma

Words and Music by
JOHN LENNON

Moderately (in 4)

Instant Karma's gonna get you,
Instant Karma's gonna get you,
gonna knock you right on the head!
gonna knock you right in the face!
You better get yourself together,
Better get yourself together,
Darlin'.
Pretty soon you're gonna be dead!
Join the human race!
What in the world you thinkin' of?
How in the world you gonna see?
Laughin' in the face of love,
Laughin' at fools like me,

Copyright © 1970 NORTHERN SONGS LIMITED, 24 Bruton Street, Mayfair, London W1X 7DA, England
All rights for the United States of America, Canada, Mexico and the Philippines controlled by
MACLEN MUSIC, INC., c/o ATV MUSIC CORP., 6255 Sunset Blvd., Hollywood, Calif. 90028
All Rights Reserved

67

what on earth you tryin' to do? It's up to you! Yeah
who on earth d'you think you are? A su-per star? Well al-
you! right you are! Well we all shine on like the
moon and the stars and the sun! Yeh, we all shine on,
ev-'ry-one, come on! In-stant Kar-ma's gon-na get you,

F
Dm
F
Dm
gon-na knock you off your feet!
Bet-ter re-cog-nise your broth-ers,
Db
Eb
F
Bb
Bb (A Bass)
Gm
Bb (F Bass)
ev-'ry-one you meet!
Why in the world are we here?
Bb
Bb (A Bass)
Gm
Bb (F Bass)
Ab
Ab (G Bass)
Fm
Ab (Eb Bass)
Sure-ly not to live in pain and fear?
Why on earth are you there?
When you're
Bb
C9
D.S. al Coda
ev-'ry-where, come and get your share!
Well we
Coda
Bb
C7
D. S. and fade-out
come on and on and on, on, on.
Well we

Julia

Moderately Slow, with a steady beat

Words and Music by
JOHN LENNON and
PAUL McCARTNEY

1. Half of what I say is mean-ing-less
2. When I can-not sing my heart

But I say it just to reach you } Ju - - - li -
I can on - ly speak my mind

1. Ju - li - a, Ju - li - a, Sea - shell eyes,
   a.
2. Ju - li - a, Sleep - ing sand,

O - cean child calls me.
Wind - y smile calls me.
Si - lent cloud touch me.

To Coda

Copyright © 1968 NORTHERN SONGS LIMITED, 24 Bruton Street, Mayfair, London W1X 7DA, England
All rights for the United States of America, Canada, Mexico and the Philippines controlled by
MACLEN MUSIC, INC., c/o ATV MUSIC CORP., 6255 Sunset Blvd., Hollywood, Calif. 90028
All Rights Reserved

So I sing a song of love, Ju - - li -
So I sing a song of love, Ju - - li -
a Her hair of float-ing sky is
shim-mer-ing, glim-mer-ing
in the sun.

D
Bm7
Am
B7
Ju - li-a,
Ju - li-a,
Morn - ing
G9
Gm7
D
Bm7
moon
touch
me.
So I sing a song of love,
F#m
A7
D
Bm
D.C. al ⊕ Coda
Ju - - li - a.
Coda
D
Bm7
F#m
D
So I sing a song of love for Ju - li - a,
F#m
D
F#m
A7
D
Ju - li - a,
Ju - - - li - a.

I Will

Words and Music by
JOHN LENNON and
PAUL McCARTNEY

Moderately

Who knows how long I've loved you, You know I love you still, Will I
if I ev - er saw you, I did - n't catch your name, But it

wait a lone - ly life - time, If you want me to I will. For
nev - er real - ly mat - tered, I will al - ways feel the

same. Love you for - ev - er and for - ev - er, Love you with all my

Copyright © 1968 NORTHERN SONGS LIMITED, 24 Bruton Street, Mayfair, London W1X 7DA, England
All rights for the United States of America, Canada, Mexico and the Philippines controlled by
MACLEN MUSIC, INC., c/o ATV MUSIC CORP., 6255 Sunset Blvd., Hollywood, Calif. 90028
All Rights Reserved

heart; Love you when-ev-er we're to-geth-er, Love you when we're a-part. And when at last I find you, Your song will fill the air, Sing it loud so I can hear you, Make it eas-y to be near you, For the things you do en-dear you to me, you know I will. I will.

Lady Madonna

Words and Music by
JOHN LENNON and
PAUL McCARTNEY

Brightly, with a beat

1.3. Lady Madonna, children at your feet, Wonder how you
2. Lady Madonna, baby at your breast, Wonders how you

3rd time To Coda

manage to make ends meet. Who finds the money
manage to feed the rest. Lady Madonna

when you pay the rent, Did you think that money was heaven sent?
lying on the bed, Listen to the music playing in your head.

Copyright © 1968 NORTHERN SONGS LIMITED, 24 Bruton Street, Mayfair, London W1X 7DA, England
All rights for the United States of America, Canada, Mexico and the Philippines controlled by
MACLEN MUSIC, INC., c/o ATV MUSIC CORP., 6255 Sunset Blvd., Hollywood, Calif. 90028
All Rights Reserved

Friday night arrives without a suitcase,
Tuesday afternoon is never ending,
Sunday morning creeping like a nun,
Wednesday morning papers didn't come,
Monday's child has learned to tie his shoelace.
Thursday night your stocking needed mending.
See how they run.

Repeat 3 times

Coda

ends meet.

Lucy in the Sky With Diamonds

Words and Music by
JOHN LENNON and
PAUL McCARTNEY

Pic - ture your - self in a boat on a riv - er with tan - ger - ine trees and mar - ma - lade skies
Fol - low her down to a bridge by a foun - tain where rock - ing horse peo - ple eat marsh - mal - low pies
Pic - ture your - self on a train in a sta - tion with plast - i - cine port - ers with look - ing - glass ties

Some - bod - y calls you, you an - swer quite
Ev' - ry - one smiles as you drift past the
Sud - den - ly some - one is there at the

Copyright © 1967 NORTHERN SONGS LIMITED, 24 Bruton Street, Mayfair, London W1X 7DA, England
All rights for the United States of America, Canada, Mexico and the Philippines controlled by
MACLEN MUSIC, INC., c/o ATV MUSIC CORP., 6255 Sunset Blvd., Hollywood, Calif. 90028
All Rights Reserved

slow-ly a girl with kal-eid-o-scope eyes.
flow-ers that grow so in-cred-ib-ly high.
turn-stile the girl with kal-eid-o-scope eyes.

Cel-lo-phane flow-ers of yel-low and
News-pa-per tax-is ap-pear on the

green tow-er-ing o-ver your head
shore wait-ing to take you a-way

Look for the girl with the sun in her eyes and she's
Climb in the back with your head in the clouds and you're

Dm G C D G C
Slow 4
gone. Lu-cy in the sky with dia monds, Lu-cy in the sky with
gone.
ff
D G C D D
D.𝄋 al Coda
dia monds, Lu-cy in the sky with dia monds Ah
CODA
Dm G C D G C
Lu-cy in the sky with dia monds, Lu-cy in the sky with
D G C D D A
dia monds, Lu-cy in the sky with dia monds, Ah
Repeat till fade

Let It Be

Words and Music by
JOHN LENNON and
PAUL McCARTNEY

Slow tempo

1. When I find my-self in times of trou-ble
2. ___ the bro-ken heart-ed peo-ple
3. *Instrumental*
4. ___ the night is cloud-y There is

Moth-er Ma-ry comes to me Speak-ing words of wis-dom, let it
Liv-ing in the world a-gree There will be an an-swer, let it
still a light that shines on me Shine un-til to-mor-row, let it

Copyright © 1970 NORTHERN SONGS LIMITED, 24 Bruton Street, Mayfair, London W1X 7DA, England
All rights for the United States of America, Canada, Mexico and the Philippines controlled by
MACLEN MUSIC, INC., c/o ATV MUSIC CORP., 6255 Sunset Blvd., Hollywood, Calif. 90028
All Rights Reserved

F C Dm7 C G
be. And in my hour of dark - ness She is
be. For though they may be part - ed there is
be. I wake up to the sound of mu - sic
Am G Fmaj7 F6 C G
stand-ing right in front of me Speak-ing words of wis - dom, let it
still a chance that they will see There will be an an - swer,
Moth-er Ma - ry comes to me Speak-ing words of wis - dom, let it
F C Dm7 C G Am G F C
be.
be.
Let it be, let it be, Let it be, let it be, (v.2. Yeah)
f
G
1.3
F C Dm7 C
Whis-per words of wis - dom, let it be.
There will be an an - swer, let it be.
Whis-per words of wis - dom, let it be.
There will be an an - swer, let it be.
2. And when
4. And when

2.4
F C Dm7 C G Am G
Let it be, let it be, let it be,
F C G
let it be, Whis-per words of wis-dom, let it be.
F C Dm7 C F Em Dm7 C B♭ F G F C
to Coda
f
F C Dm C G F C
D.% al Coda
(Instrumental and Repeat)
CODA
G F G C

The Long and Winding Road

Words and Music by
JOHN LENNON and
PAUL McCARTNEY

The long and wind-ing road that leads to your door
wild and wind-y night that the rain washed a-way

will nev-er dis-ap-pear, I've seen that road be-fore,
has left a pool of tears cry-ing for the day,

It al-ways leads me here,
Why leave me stand-ing here,

lead me to your door. The
let me know the way.

Copyright © 1970 NORTHERN SONGS LIMITED, 24 Bruton Street, Mayfair, London W1X 7DA, England
All rights for the United States of America, Canada, Mexico and the Philippines controlled by
Maclen Music, Inc., c/o ATV MUSIC CORP., 6255 Sunset Blvd., Hollywood, Calif. 90028
All Rights Reserved

Many times I've been alone and many times I've cried, Anyway you'll never know the many ways I've tried but still they lead me back to the long winding road, You left me standing here, a long long time ago, Don't leave me waiting here, lead me to your door. Da da da da.

Magical Mystery Tour

Words and Music by
JOHN LENNON and
PAUL McCARTNEY

G
1. To make a res - er - va - tion
2. Sat-is - fac - tion guar - an - teed.
B♭
C
Last time To Coda
Roll up,
Roll up for the mys - te - ry tour.
F
Fmaj7
F7
B♭
F+
The ma - gi - cal mys - te - ry tour is wait - ing to take you a - way,
The ma - gi - cal mys - te - ry tour is hop - ing to take you a - way,
F
C7
Coda
Wait - ing to take you a - way.
Hop - ing to take you a - way.
D.S. al Coda
The ma - gi - cal mys - te - ry tour is com - ing to take you a -
The ma - gi - cal mys - te - ry tour is dy - ing to take you a -
way, Com - ing to take you a - way.
way, Dy - ing to take you a - way, take you a - way.

Maxwell's Silver Hammer

Words and Music by
JOHN LENNON and
PAUL McCARTNEY

Moderately Bright

Joan was quiz-zi-cal Stud-ied pat-a-phys-i-cal science in the home. Late nights all a-lone with a test tube Oh, oh, oh, oh. Max-well Ed-i-son Ma-jor-ing in med-i-cine,

Back in school a-gain, Max-well plays the fool a-gain Teach-er gets an-noyed. Wish-ing to a-void an un-pleas-ant sce-e-e-ene. She tells Max to stay when the class has gone a-way,

P. C. Thir-ty-one said, "We've caught a dir-ty one," Max-well stands a-lone. Paint-ing test-i-mon-i-al pic-tures, Oh, oh, oh, oh. Rose and Val-er-ie Scream-ing from the gal-ler-y

Copyright © 1969 NORTHERN SONGS LIMITED, 24 Bruton Street, Mayfair, London W1X 7DA, England
All rights for the United States of America, Canada, Mexico and the Philippines controlled by
MACLEN MUSIC, INC., c/o ATV MUSIC CORP., 6255 Sunset Blvd., Hollywood, Calif. 90028
All Rights Reserved

calls her on the phone; "Can I take you out to the pic - tures, Jo -
So he waits be - hind, Writ-ing fif - ty times, "I must not be so -
Say he must go free. The judge does not a - gree, and he tells them so -

o - o - oan?___ But, as she's get - ting read - y to go,___ A knock comes on the door.
o - o - o."___ But, when she turns her back on the boy,___ He creeps up from be - hind.
o - o - o.___ But, as the words are leav - ing his lips,___ A noise comes from be - hind.

Bang! Bang! Max - well's Sil - ver Ham - mer came down up - on her head.___
Bang! Bang! Max - well's Sil - ver Ham - mer came down up - on her head.___

To Coda ✛

Clang! Clang! Max-well's Sil-ver Ham-mer made
sure that she was dead.

Bang! Bang! Max-well's Sil-ver Ham-mer came down up-on his head.
Clang! Clang! Max-well's Sil-ver Ham-mer made sure that he was dead.

Maybe I'm Amazed

Words and Music by
PAUL McCARTNEY

89

1. Ba-by I'm a-mazed at the way you
3. May-be I'm a-mazed at the way you're
2-4: *Instrumental ad lib solo*

love me all the time, And may-be I'm a-fraid of the way I
with me all the time, And may-be I'm a-fraid of the way I

love you.
need you.

May-be I'm a-mazed at the way you
May-be I'm a-mazed at the way you

Copyright © 1970 NORTHERN SONGS LIMITED, 24 Bruton Street, Mayfair, London W1X 7DA, England
All rights for the United States of America, Canada, Mexico and the Philippines controlled by
MACLEN MUSIC, INC., c/o ATV MUSIC CORP., 6255 Sunset Blvd., Hollywood, Calif. 90028
All Rights Reserved

pulled me out of time,_ hung me on a line,_
help me sing my song,_ right me when I'm wrong,_ And

may-be I'm a-mazed at the way I real - ly need you._

4th time to Coda ⊕

Ba - by, I'm a man, may-be I'm a lone - ly man_ who's in the mid-dle of some - thing_

that he does-n't real - ly un - der - stand._

Ba-by, I'm a man, and may-be you're the on-ly wom-an who could ev-er help me;

Ba-by, won't you help me to un-der-stand? Oo _____

D.S. 𝄋 al Coda

3rd time rit.

Coda

(Keep repeating with ad lib guitar figures till fade)

Mother Nature's Son

Words and Music by
JOHN LENNON and
PAUL McCARTNEY

Moderato

1. Born a poor young country boy, Mother Nature's son, All day long I'm sitting singing songs for ev'ry-one.
2. Sit beside a mountain stream, See her waters rise; Listen to the pretty sound of music as she flies.
3. Find me in my field of grass, Mother Nature's son. Swaying daisies sing a lazy song beneath the sun.

Copyright © 1968 NORTHERN SONGS LIMITED, 24 Bruton Street, Mayfair, London W1X 7DA, England
All rights for the United States of America, Canada, Mexico and the Philippines controlled by
MACLEN MUSIC, INC., c/o ATV MUSIC CORP., 6255 Sunset Blvd., Hollywood, Calif. 90028
All Rights Reserved

1.
Eb
Bb
Bbm7
Eb
Bb
2.
Bb
To next strain
Du du
3.
Bb
Bbm7
Eb
Bb
Fine
Hm hm Mother Nature's son.
rit.
Bb
Eb
1. Bb
2. Bb
Bbmaj7
du du du du du du du du. du
mf
Bb7
Bb11
Bb7
Eb
Ebm
Bb
D. S. al Fine
du du du.

Ob-la-di, Ob-la-da

Words and Music by
JOHN LENNON and
PAUL McCARTNEY

Bright Tempo

Des-mond had a bar-row in the mar-ket place ___ Mol-ly is the
Des-mond takes a trol-ley to the jewel-er's store ___ buys ___ a twen-ty
Hap-py ev-er af-ter in the mar-ket place ___ Des-mond lets the

sing-er in a band. Des-mond says to Mol-ly girl I
ca-rat gold-en ring. Takes ___ it back to Mol-ly wait-ing
child-ren lend a hand. Mol-ly stays at home and does her

like your face ___ and Mol-ly says this as she takes him by the hand. ___
at the door ___ and as he gives it to her she be-gins to sing. ___
pret-ty face ___ and in the eve-ning she still sings it with the band. ___

Copyright © 1968 NORTHERN SONGS LIMITED, 24 Bruton Street, Mayfair, London W1X 7DA, England
All rights for the United States of America, Canada, Mexico and the Philippines controlled by
MACLEN MUSIC, INC., c/o ATV MUSIC CORP., 6255 Sunset Blvd., Hollywood, Calif. 90028
All Rights Reserved

Dm
Gm
Ob - la - di Ob - la - da life goes on bra la
Bb
F7
Bb
la how the life goes on. Ob - la - di Ob - la - da
Dm
Gm
Bb
F7
To Coda
life goes on bra la la how the life goes on.
Bb
1.
2.
Bb
Eb
In a cou-ple of years they have

built a home sweet home

with a couple of kids running in the yard of Des-mond and Mol-ly Jones.

and if you want some fun take ob-la-di-bla-da.

Oh! Darling

Words and Music by
JOHN LENNON and
PAUL McCARTNEY

Slowly

Oh! Darling, Please believe me, I'll never do you no harm. Believe me when I tell you, I'll never do you no harm. Oh! Darling, If you leave me,

Copyright © 1969 NORTHERN SONGS LIMITED, 24 Bruton Street, Mayfair, London W1X 7DA, England
All rights for the United States of America, Canada, Mexico and the Philippines controlled by
MACLEN MUSIC, INC., c/o ATV MUSIC CORP., 6255 Sunset Blvd., Hollywood, Calif. 90028
All Rights Reserved

98

I'll nev-er make it__ a-lone.__ Be-lieve me when I beg you,__

Don't ev-er leave me__ a-lone.__ When you

told me__ you did-n't need me an-y-more,__ Well, you

know I near-ly broke down__ and cried.__ When you told me__ you did-n't

need me an-y-more,___ Well, you know I near-ly broke down___ and died.___ Oh!___
Oh!___

Dar - ling,___ if you leave me,___ I'll nev - er make it___ a -
Dar - ling,___ Please be - lieve me,___ I'll nev - er let___ you

lone.___ Be - lieve me when I tell you,___ I'll nev - er do you___ no
down.___ Be - lieve me when I tell you,___ I'll nev - er do you___ no

harm.___
harm.___ When you

Penny Lane

**Words and Music by
JOHN LENNON and
PAUL McCARTNEY**

Moderate Ragtime feeling

Pen-ny Lane: There is a bar-ber show-ing pho-to-graphs of ev-'ry head he's had the pleas-ure to know.
(Last time) shel-ter in the mid-dle of the round-a-bout a pret-ty nurse is sell-ing pop-pies from a

tray. And all the peo-ple that come and go stop and say hel-lo.
And tho' she feels as if she's in a play she is an-y-way.

On the cor-ner is a bank-er with a mo-tor car. The lit-tle chil-dren laugh at him be-hind his
Lane: there is a fire-man with an hour glass. And in his pock-et is a por-trait of the
Pen-ny Lane: the bar-ber shaves an-oth-er cus-tom-er. We see the bank-er sit-ting, wait-ing for a

back. And the bank-er nev-er wears a "mac"* in the pour-ing rain, ver-y
queen. He likes to keep his fi-re en-gine clean, it's a clean ma-chine,
trend. And then the fi-re-man rush-es in from the pour-ing rain, ver-y

*British slang for "raincoat".

Copyright © 1967 NORTHERN SONGS LIMITED, 24 Bruton Street, Mayfair, London W1X 7DA, England
All rights for the United States of America, Canada, Mexico and the Philippines controlled by
MACLEN MUSIC, INC., c/o ATV MUSIC CORP., 6255 Sunset Blvd., Hollywood, Calif. 90028
All Rights Reserved

Eb
Ab
Cm
Db
strange!
strange!
Pen-ny Lane is in my ears and in my eyes.
Ab
Cm
Db
To Coda
Adim
F7
1. 3. Wet be-neath the blue sub-urb-an skies. I sit and... mean-while, back in Pen-ny
2. full of fish and fin-ger pies in sum-mer mean-while, back be-hind the
Last time D. S. al Coda
Coda
Adim
F7
Bb
Dm
mean-while back... Pen-ny Lane is in my ears and in my eyes
Eb
Bb
Dm
wet be-neath the blue sub-urb-an skies.
Eb
Bb
Pen-ny Lane.

Revolution

Words and Music by
JOHN LENNON and
PAUL McCARTNEY

Moderate Tempo

You say you want a re-vo-lu-tion, _____ Well _____ you know, _____
say you got a real so-lu-tion, _____ Well _____ you know, _____
say you'll change the con-sti-tu-tion, _____ Well _____ you know, _____

We all want _____ to change the world. You
We'd all love _____ to see the plan. You
We all want _____ to change your head. You

tell me that it's e-vo-lu-tion, _____ Well _____ you know, _____
ask me for a con-tri-bu-tion, _____ Well _____ you know, _____
tell me it's the in-sti-tu-tion, _____ Well _____ you know, _____

Copyright © 1968 NORTHERN SONGS LIMITED, 24 Bruton Street, Mayfair, London W1X 7DA, England
All rights for the United States of America, Canada, Mexico and the Philippines controlled by
MACLEN MUSIC, INC., c/o ATV MUSIC CORP., 6255 Sunset Blvd., Hollywood, Calif. 90028
All Rights Reserved

We all want to change the world.
We're do - ing what we can.
You bet - ter free your mind in - stead.

But when you talk a - bout de - struc - tion,
But when you want mon - ey for peo - ple with minds that hate,
But if you go car - ry - ing pic - tures of Chair - man Mao,

Don't you know that you can count me out.
All I can tell you is broth - er you have to wait.
You ain't going to make it with an - y - one an - y - how.

Don't you know it's gon - na be al - right,

C
F6
C
al - right,
al - right.
F6
G11
C
C
G7
1. 2.
3.
You
You
Al - right,
C
F
C
F
al - right,
al - right,
al - right,
al - right,
C
F
G7
C
al - right,
al - right,
al - right.
3
3

Rocky Raccoon

Words and Music by
JOHN LENNON and
PAUL McCARTNEY

Moderately

Spoken: Now somewhere in the Black Mountain hills of Dakota there lived a young boy named Rocky Raccoon,

And one day his woman ran off with another guy; Hit young Rocky in the eye; Rocky didn't like that.

He said, "I'm going to get that boy." So one day he walked into town and booked himself a room in a local saloon.

Copyright © 1968 NORTHERN SONGS LIMITED, 24 Bruton Street, Mayfair, London W1X 7DA, England
All rights for the United States of America, Canada, Mexico and the Philippines controlled by
MACLEN MUSIC, INC., c/o ATV MUSIC CORP., 6255 Sunset Blvd., Hollywood, Calif. 90028
All Rights Reserved

1. Rock-y Rac-coon checked in-to his room on-ly to find Gid-eon's Bi-ble.
Rock-y had come e-quipped with a gun to shoot off the legs of his ri-val. His

She and her man who called him-self Dan were in the next room at the hoe-down.
Rock-y burst in and grin-ning a grin, He said, "Dan-ny boy, this is a show-down." But

ri-val it seems had brok-en his dreams by
name was Ma-gill, she called her-self Lil, But

steal-ing the girl of his fan-cy. Her
ev-'ry-one knew her as Nan-cy. 2. Now

Dan-iel was hot, he drew first and shot and

Rock-y col-lapsed in the cor-ner.

3. Now the doctor came in stinking of gin and proceeded to lie on the table.
   He said, "Rocky you met your match." And Rocky said, "Doc, it's only a scratch,
   And I'll be better, I'll be better Doc, as soon as I'm able."

4. Now Rocky Raccoon, he fell back in his room only to find Gideon's Bible.
   Gideon checked out and he left it no doubt to help with good Rocky's revival.

Sgt. Pepper's Lonely Hearts Club Band

Words and Music by
JOHN LENNON and
PAUL McCARTNEY

109

Ser-geant Pep-per's Lone-ly Hearts Club Band.

Fine

CHORUS We're Ser-geant Pep-per's Lone-ly Hearts Club Band, We hope you will en-joy the show. We're Ser-geant Pep-per's Lone-ly Hearts Club Band. Sit back and let the eve-ning go,

LAST CHORUS

We're Sgt. Pepper's lonely hearts club band
We hope you have enjoyed the show
We're Sgt. Pepper's lonely hearts club band
We're sorry but it's time to go
Sgt. Pepper's lonely, Sgt. Pepper's lonely,
Sgt. Pepper's lonely hearts club band
We'd like to thank you once again
Sgt. Pepper's one and only
Lonely hearts club band
It's getting very near the end.
Sgt. Pepper's lonely hearts club band.

She's Leaving Home

**Words and Music by
JOHN LENNON and
PAUL McCARTNEY**

Wedn's-day morn-ing at five o'-clock as the day be-gins___
Fa-ther snores as his wife gets in-to her dres-sing gown___

Sil-ent-ly clos-ing her bed-room door___
Picks up the let-ter that's ly-ing there___

Leav-ing the note that she hoped would say more She goes
Stand-ing a-lone at the top of the stairs She breaks

Copyright © 1967 NORTHERN SONGS LIMITED, 24 Bruton Street, Mayfair, London W1X 7DA, England
All rights for the United States of America, Canada, Mexico and the Philippines controlled by
MACLEN MUSIC, INC., c/o ATV MUSIC CORP., 6255 Sunset Blvd., Hollywood, Calif. 90028
All Rights Reserved

down - stairs to the kit - chen clutch-ing her hand - ker-chief
down and cries to her hus - band Dad - dy our ba - by's gone
Fri - day morn - ing at nine o' clock she is far a - way

Qui - et - ly turn - ing the back - door key
Why would she treat us so thought-less-ly
Wait - ing to keep the ap - point - ment she

Step - ping out - side she is free
How could she do this to me
made Meet - ing a man from the mo - tor trade

She (We gave her most of our lives) is leav-ing (Sac - ri - ficed
(We ne - ver thought of our selves) (Nev - er a
She (What did we do that was wrong) is hav-ing (We did - n't

Bm6
To Coda
most of our lives) Home (We gave her ev - 'ry-thing mo - ney could
thought for our selves) (We strug - gled hard all our lives to get
know it was wrong) (Fun is the one thing that mo - ney can't
C#m
F#7
C#m
She's leav - ing home af - ter liv-ing a - lone for so man - y years
buy Bye - bye)
by Bye - bye)
F#7
D.S. al Coda
CODA
C#m
F#7
Some-thing in - side that was al - ways de-nied for so
buy Bye -
C#m7
F#7
C#m
man - y years She's leav - ing
bye
F#7
A
E
home Bye - bye

She Came in Through the Bathroom Window

Moderately Slow

Words and Music by
JOHN LENNON and
PAUL McCARTNEY

She came in through the bath-room win-dow,___ Pro-tect-ed by a sil-ver
And so I quit the Police De-part-ment, And got my-self a stead-y

spoon.___
job.___

But now she sucks her thumb and won-ders___ By the
And though she tried her best to help me,___ She could

banks of her own la-goon.___ Did-n't an-y-bod-y tell___ her?
steal, but she could not rob.

Did-n't an-y-bod-y see?___ Sun-days on the phone to Mon-day;

To Coda

Copyright © 1969 NORTHERN SONGS LIMITED, 24 Bruton Street, Mayfair, London W1X 7DA, England
All rights for the United States of America, Canada, Mexico and the Philippines controlled by
MACLEN MUSIC, INC., c/o ATV MUSIC CORP., 6255 Sunset Blvd., Hollywood, Calif. 90028
All Rights Reserved

Tues-days on the phone to me,_____ She said she'd al- ways been a dan-cer,_____ She worked at fif- teen clubs a day._____ And though she thought I knew the ans-wer;_____ Well, I knew what I could not say._____

Coda

Tues-days on the phone to me._____ Oh, yeah._____

Strawberry Fields Forever

Words and Music by
JOHN LENNON and
PAUL McCARTNEY

Andante

Let me take you down__ cause I'm go-in' to__ straw-ber-ry fields. Nothing is real. and nothing to get hung a-bout Straw-ber-ry fields for - ev - er.__

Liv-ing is eas-y with eyes closed.__ Mis - un - der - stand-ing all you see.__
No one I think is in my tree.__ I mean it must be high or low.__
Al - ways know, some-times think it's me, But you know I know and it's a dream.

Copyright © 1967 NORTHERN SONGS LIMITED, 24 Bruton Street, Mayfair, London W1X 7DA, England
All rights for the United States of America, Canada, Mexico and the Philippines controlled by
MACLEN MUSIC, INC., c/o ATV MUSIC CORP., 6255 Sunset Blvd., Hollywood, Calif. 90028
All Rights Reserved

It's get-ting hard to be some - one but it all works out It does-n't mat-ter much to me.
That is, you know you can't tune in but it's all right that is, I think it's not too bad.
I think I know of thee, ah, yes but it's all wrong that is, I think I dis - a - gree.

Let me take you down 'cause I'm go-ing to straw-ber-ry fields. No-thing is real, and no-thing to get hung a-bout... Straw-ber-ry fields for-ev-er.

Repeat and fade

That Would Be Something

Words and Music by
PAUL McCARTNEY

Moderately slow

That would be some-thing__ It real-ly would be some-thing__

That would be some-thing__ To meet you in the fall-ing rain.__ Mom-ma

Copyright © 1970 NORTHERN SONGS LIMITED, 24 Bruton Street, Mayfair, London W1X 7DA, England
All rights for the United States of America, Canada, Mexico and the Philippines controlled by
MACLEN MUSIC, INC., c/o ATV MUSIC CORP., 6255 Sunset Blvd., Hollywood, Calif. 90028
All Rights Reserved

G
B♭
D
F
meet you in the fall - ing rain
Oo hm hm
Oo hm hm
Oo hm hm
G
B♭
D
F
G
B♭
D
F
Meet you in the fall - ing rain
Mom-ma
meet you in the fall - ing rain
G
B♭
D
F
D7
F7
G
B♭
A9sus4
C9sus4
D
F
D7
F7
Meet you in the fall - ing rain
Mom-ma
Meet you in the fall - ing rain

You Never Give Me Your Money

Words and Music by
JOHN LENNON and
PAUL McCARTNEY

Slowly

[Am7]   [Dm]   [G7]

1. You nev-er give me your mo-ney___ You on-ly give me your
2. I nev-er give you my num-ber___ I on-ly give you my

Small notes 2nd time (Bass Gtr.)

[C]   [Fmaj7]   [Dm6]   [E7]

fun-ny pa-per   And in the mid-dle of ne-go-ti-a-tions you
sit-u-a-tion   And in the mid-dle of in-ves-ti-ga-tion I

Copyright © 1969 NORTHERN SONGS LIMITED, 24 Bruton Street, Mayfair, London W1X 7DA, England
All rights for the United States of America, Canada, Mexico and the Philippines controlled by
Maclen Music, INC., c/o ATV MUSIC CORP., 6255 Sunset Blvd., Hollywood, Calif. 90028
All Rights Reserved

Am
break down.
break down.
1.
2. C G7
C E7 Am C7
Out of col-lege mo-ney spent See no fu-ture pay no rent
An-y Job-ber got the sack Mon-day morn-ing turn-ing back
F G7
1. C
All the mo-ney's gone no-where to go.
Yel-low lor-ry slow no-where to go.
2. C
Bb
But oh that ma-gic feel-ing
Oh that ma-gic feel-ing

122

no - where to go.
no - where to go. _____ _____ no - where to go _____

Ah _____

Ah _____ Ah   Ah

Ah

One sweet dream___ Pick up the bags and get in the lim-ou-sine___

Soon we'll be a-way___ from here___ Step on the gas and wipe___ that tear a-way___

One sweet dream___ came true___ to-day___

came true___ to-day.___

One, two, three, four, five, six, sev-en,

All good child-ren go to heav-en.

Ad lib. Instrumental Solo

Keep repeating till fade

When I'm Sixty-Four

Words and Music by
JOHN LENNON and
PAUL McCARTNEY

Medium tempo

3 Times

When I get old-er los-ing my hair, ma-ny years from now, will you still be send-ing me a val-en-tine, birth-day greet-ings, bot-tle of wine.
I could be hand-y mend-ing a fuse when your lights have gone, you can knit a sweat-er by the fire-side, Sun-day morn-ings, go for a ride.
Send me a post-card drop me a line stat-ing point of view, in-di-cate pre-cise-ly what you mean to say, yours sin-cere-ly wast-ing a-way

Tacet--------*

Copyright © 1967 NORTHERN SONGS LIMITED, 24 Bruton Street, Mayfair, London W1X 7DA, England
All rights for the United States of America, Canada, Mexico and the Philippines controlled by
MACLEN MUSIC, INC., c/o ATV MUSIC CORP., 6255 Sunset Blvd., Hollywood, Calif. 90028
All Rights Reserved

If I'd been out till quarter to three would you lock the door
doing the gar - den dig - ging the weeds Who could ask for more
Give me your an - swer fill in a form Mine for ev - er more

Will you still need me, will you still feed me, when I'm six-ty - four.

(Tacet 1st)
2nd. Ev'- ry sum-mer we can rent a cot-tage in the Isle of Wight 1st. Oo

if it's not too dear. You'll be old - er
We shall scrimp and (Ah
(We shall scrimp and

too. Ah — And if you
save —
save

say the word — I could stay with
on your knee — Vera, Chuck and

you
Dave

CODA

-four. (Ho!)